Alfresco
Dining

Notes

1. Standard level spoon and cup measurements are used in all recipes.
1 tablespoon = 3 teaspoons
1 cup = 8 fl oz

2. Eggs should be large unless otherwise stated. The Surgeon General advises that eggs should not be consumed raw. This book contains dishes made with raw or lightly cooked eggs. It is prudent for more vulnerable people, such as pregnant and nursing mothers, invalids, the elderly, babies and young children, and those with an impaired immune system, to avoid uncooked or lightly cooked dishes made with eggs. Once prepared, these dishes should be kept refrigerated and used promptly.

3. Milk should be whole milk unless otherwise stated.

4. Fresh herbs should be used unless otherwise stated. If unavailable, use dried herbs as an alternative but halve the quantities stated.

5. Ovens should be preheated to the specified temperature—if using a fan-assisted oven, follow the manufacturer's instructions for adjusting the time and the temperature.

6. Pepper should be freshly ground black pepper unless otherwise stated.

7. This book includes dishes made with nuts and nut derivatives. It is advisable for readers with known allergic reactions to nuts and nut derivatives and those who may be potentially vulnerable to these allergies, such as pregnant and nursing mothers, invalids, the elderly, babies, and children, to avoid dishes made with nuts and nut oils. It is also prudent to check the labels of pre-prepared ingredients for the possible inclusion of nut derivatives.

Alfresco Dining

text Marie Abadie

photographs Jean-Pierre Dieterlen

design Marianne Paquin

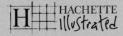
HACHETTE
Illustrated

preface

Going on a picnic is like embarking on an adventure trip with your dining room tucked firmly under your arm. At the end of the trail, a corner of nature awaits you. Look, how about there? On that shady bank by the stream? Like an invading army, you quickly stake your claim, spread your cloth on an imaginary table, and set it with real food. A picnic means leaving table manners locked in the closet—to the delight of the child inside us all. It means dispensing with cutlery and eating with your fingers, shedding inhibitions, forgetting about diets, and just enjoying it all.

Picnicking is a part of being on vacation. So, here I have filled my baskets with produce from everywhere, as each season offers its bounty.

Lunch on the grass in June, on boat trips or in a shady wood; a menu to please weekend painters, or lovers; cherries playfully worn as earrings and cherries baked in a batter. In summer, tortillas, shrimp with pimientos, and sangría are in perfect harmony with the waves on an Atlantic beach. Sheltering from the wind in a gray-blue rocky inlet? That's just the right moment to open up the hamper and bring out an olive and thyme bread, still warm from the oven. On a coastal road in the fall, the smell of a citrus-flavored cake will mingle temptingly with the mist.

Marie Abadie

fishing trips and lakesides

Festive tomatoes
with tartar sauce, guacamole, and cottage cheese fillings

Preparation time:
30 min

Serves 6

2 pounds cherry vine tomatoes

2 tablespoons capers

4 tablespoons lemon juice

$1/2$ teaspoon grated lemon rind

$1/2$ bunch chervil

$1/2$ cup mayonnaise

1 avocado

Tabasco sauce

3 tablespoons olive oil

$1/2$ cup cottage cheese

1 mint sprig

salt, pepper

1. Remove the tomatoes from the vine, leaving just the flower stalk attached, and put in an airtight container.

2. Put the fillings in separate jars. Before serving, hollow out the tomatoes and stuff with the fillings.

Tartar sauce
1. Chop the capers, add a little lemon juice, the grated lemon rind, and 2 tablespoons chopped chervil.

2. Combine these ingredients with the mayonnaise. Season to taste with salt and pepper.

Guacamole
1. Pour the remaining lemon juice into a bowl, reserving 1 teaspoonful.

2. Peel, pit, and slice the avocado. Add to the bowl with salt and pepper, a dash of Tabasco, and 2 tablespoons of olive oil. Mash coarsely with a fork and mix thoroughly.

Cottage cheese with herbs
1. Mash the cottage cheese with a fork. Coarsely chop 2 tablespoons of chervil and mint leaves.

2. Combine with the teaspoon of lemon juice and 1 tablespoon of olive oil. Season with salt and pepper.

Trout pâté

Preparation time:
20 min

Cooking time: 10 min

Makes 2 pots,
each 12 ounces

2 bay leaves

2 thyme sprigs

2 garlic cloves, peeled

pink peppercorns

7 tablespoons white distilled vinegar

1 pound fresh trout fillets

olive oil

2 smoked trout fillets, skinned

salt, pepper

1. To cook the fresh trout fillets, put 2 teaspoons of salt, the bay leaves, thyme sprigs, garlic, and a few pink peppercorns into 4 cups of water and bring to a boil, then add the vinegar.

2. Boil gently for 5 minutes before adding the trout fillets. With the water barely simmering, poach the fish for about 5 minutes, or until the flesh flakes easily with the point of a knife.

3. Drain off the liquid, retaining the garlic but discarding the herbs and peppercorns. Remove any remaining bones and the skin from the fish.

4. Put the flesh into a food processor together with the garlic. With the processor running, add olive oil, drop by drop, until the mixture is smooth and creamy. Scrape into a bowl.

5. Mash the smoked trout fillets with a fork and stir into the fresh trout mixture, together with a few more pink peppercorns. Season to taste with salt and pepper.

6. Spoon the pâté into ramekins or pots, cover with plastic wrap, and store in the refrigerator until required.

TASTE BITE

SPREAD THIS PÂTÉ on little round rolls, or on rye bread, with scallions, salad greens, and a few slices of fresh tomato.

TIP

THE WHITE DISTILLED VINEGAR in this pâté means that it will keep fresh in the refrigerator for 10 days or so, but check on it each day. This recipe can also be used for salmon or fresh and smoked mackerel.

Sunday-best chicken marinated in spices

Preparation time:
25 min

Marinate: 1 hour

Cooking time: 50 min

Serves 6

For the chicken

4 tablespoons sour cream

2 tablespoons ground turmeric

1 teaspoon ground cumin

1 oven-ready chicken, about 3 pounds

1 rosemary sprig

1 lime, sliced

1 teaspoon olive oil

salt, pepper

For the sauce

$^2/_3$ cup plain yogurt

1 cup lemon mayonnaise

2 teaspoons ground turmeric

$^1/_4$ teaspoon cayenne pepper

salt, pepper

1. Combine the sour cream, spices, and a generous pinch of freshly ground pepper in a bowl to make a marinade.

2. Put 2 tablespoons of the marinade inside the chicken with the rosemary and slices of lime.

3. Spread the rest of the marinade all over the chicken and set aside for 1 hour.

4. Preheat the oven to 400°F. Drizzle the olive oil over the chicken, season it with salt, and roast for 50 minutes, or until the juices run golden and clear when the point of a knife is inserted.

5. Remove the chicken from the oven, stand it on a plate and baste with the cooking juices, which should be nicely colored. Let it rest for 15 minutes before carving.

6. Combine all the sauce ingredients in a bowl and season to taste with salt and pepper.

 TASTE BITE

PROVIDE LARGE SLICES of bread, a dish of sliced cucumber, some salad greens, and scallions.

TIP

IF YOU LIKE, this dish can be made with chicken breast portions (one per person). To keep them moist and prevent them from shrinking, place in cold oil in a roasting pan, put in the oven, and bring up to temperature in Step 4. Turn the portions over frequently and add the marinade after they have been cooking for about 3–4 minutes.

Weekend artist's roast

Preparation time:
20 min

Cooking time: 1 hour

Serves 6

**1 cup pitted
green olives**

**rolled tenderloin of
pork, with the skin
removed, about
2¹/₂ pounds**

olive oil

paprika

cayenne pepper

1 cup cream cheese

**1 small bunch
cilantro, coarsely
chopped**

salt, pepper

1. Rinse the olives, dry them on paper towels, and cut in half lengthwise.

2. With a sharp, pointed knife, make fairly deep cuts over the whole surface of the meat and push in the olives. Reserve 12 olives to add to the sauce.

3. Preheat the oven to 400°F. Brush the meat all over with olive oil and sprinkle generously with paprika and cayenne pepper to color the surface bright orange.

4. Roast for 20 minutes, then lower the oven temperature to 350°F, and roast for 40 minutes more. Check that the juices run clear when the point of a knife is inserted. Set aside to cool.

5. Make the sauce by mixing the remaining olives with the cream cheese. Add the cilantro and season to taste with salt, black pepper, and cayenne pepper.

TIP
TO AVOID MAKING excessively large cuts in the meat, use small olives. The dish can also be made with black or purple olives. Wait until the meat is completely cold before carving, and place it on a sheet of waxed paper to catch the juices.

Gardener's quiche

Preparation time:
35 min

Chilling: 30 min

Cooking time: 50 min

Serves 6

8 ounces ready-made puff pastry dough, thawed if frozen

2 pounds fresh peas in the pod

8 ounces snow peas

1 tablespoon butter

1 small egg white

1 tablespoon potato flour

3 tablespoons light cream

4 eggs

2¹/₂–3 ounces soft goat cheese

1¹/₂ cups cream cheese

1 tablespoon chopped chives

salt, pepper

 TIP

THE EGG WHITE coats the pastry and prevents it from absorbing any liquid given off by the vegetables during baking. Only a small amount of egg white is used.

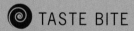 TASTE BITE

THIS QUICHE is the perfect accompaniment for cold meats. For the quintessential flavor of summer in the yard, add a bowl of freshly picked young fava beans, removed from the pods, and boiled until tender but still firm to the bite.

1. Line a 10-inch quiche pan with the puff pastry and chill in the refrigerator for 30 minutes.

2. Shuck the peas, trim the snow peas, and cut them into strips.

3. Blanch the peas for 3 minutes in 4 cups boiling water and blanch the snow peas for 3–4 minutes. Put them into a bowl with the butter, mix well, and set aside.

4. Lightly beat the egg white to slacken it and brush a thin layer over the pastry. Leave it to dry.

5. Preheat the oven to 350°F. Combine the potato flour and cream in a small pan, stir over low heat for a few seconds to thicken it, then transfer to a food processor. Add the eggs, goat cheese, and cream cheese and process until smooth. Season with salt and pepper.

6. Arrange the vegetables on the pie shell and pour the egg mixture over them. Sprinkle with chives.

7. Place the quiche on a cookie sheet and bake for about 40 minutes, until well risen and the top is golden brown.

Jumbo shrimp and trout pies

Preparation time:
30 min

Chilling: 10 min

Cooking time: 25 min

Makes 6 individual
pies

**8 ounces trout
fillets**

all-purpose flour

**5 tablespoons olive
oil**

**1 pound raw jumbo
shrimp, thawed if
frozen**

**3 shallots, finely
chopped**

**1 garlic clove,
crushed**

**1 bunch chives,
finely chopped**

**1 bunch tarragon,
finely chopped**

**1 cup flowery
white wine**

**2 tablespoons
butter**

**ready-made puff
pastry, thawed if
frozen**

cayenne pepper

1 egg, beaten

salt, pepper

1. Cut the fish fillets into strips and dust lightly with flour.

2. Heat 1 tablespoon of the olive oil in a pan and cook the fish strips, skin side down, for 1 minute, season with salt and pepper, and set aside.

3. Add the remaining oil to the pan. Cook the shrimp for 3–4 minutes, stirring frequently, then season with salt and pepper and a few pinches of cayenne. Reserve the oil in the pan.

4. Peel the shrimp and remove the intestinal tract. Reserve the heads. Brown the shallots in the reserved oil. Add the shrimp heads, garlic, 1 tablespoon each of the herbs, the white wine, and scant 1 cup water.

5. Reduce the liquid by half, then rub the mixture through a strainer to produce a thick, creamy sauce. Add the butter and the rest of the herbs. Set aside to cool.

6. Preheat the oven to 425°F. Roll out the dough on a floured surface, and use to line six individual quiche pans, leaving a margin of dough overhanging the rims. Chill in the freezer for 10 minutes.

7. Arrange the shrimp and the strips of trout in the pie shells. Add the herb mixture. Fold over the overhanging pastry neatly to make a lid and seal with beaten egg. Bake the tarts for 12 minutes.

TIP

CRAYFISH could take the place of the jumbo shrimp.

TASTE BITE

PLACE ANCHOVY FILLETS on any dough that is left over. Cut into strips and bake for 5 minutes. These make excellent and unusual anchovy straws.

Cone of shortbread bars with berry ratafia

Preparation time:

The ratafia: 20 min, 5 days before

Cooking time: 10 min

The shortbread: 10 min, the day before

Cooking time:
The ratafia: 10 min

The shortbread: 12 min

Serves 6

For the ratafia

4 cups berries (black currants, red currants, raspberries)

1 cup superfine sugar

scant 1 cup white wine

1 peppermint sprig

7 tablespoons crème de cassis (black currant liqueur)

For the shortbread

1 egg

$^1/_2$ cup granulated sugar, plus extra for dredging

1 teaspoon grated lemon rind

$^2/_3$ cup butter, softened

2 cups all-purpose flour

1. Prepare the ratafia 5 days in advance. Wash the berries and drain them on paper towels.

2. Stir the sugar into the wine and bring to a boil. Add the berries and the mint. Bring back to a boil, lower the heat, and simmer gently for 5 minutes, then remove from the heat, and leave to soak overnight.

3. Next day, cook the mixture for 10 minutes, add the black currant liqueur, discard the mint, and put the mixture into jars. Cover immediately.

4. Prepare the shortbread cookies the day before they are needed. Beat the egg with the sugar and the lemon rind in a bowl. Beat in the butter, then the flour, a little at a time.

5. Knead the dough lightly with the tips of your fingers, then form it into a ball, cover with plastic wrap, and place in the refrigerator.

6. The next day, preheat the oven to 400°F. Roll out the dough to $^1/_2$ inch thick and cut into bars the size of large French fries.

7. Bake for 10–12 minutes on a nonstick or greased cookie sheet. Leave to cool completely on a wire rack before dredging with sugar and storing in an airtight container.

TASTE BITE
THIS SHORTBREAD ALSO TASTES GOOD with a coulis of red berry fruits or fromage blanc/mascarpone cheese.

 TIP
RATAFIA is a sweet liqueur made with fruits soaked in eau-de-vie. This version is based on it but, unlike that made to the traditional recipe, it will not keep for more than 3 weeks in the refrigerator.

Cherry clafoutis

Preparation time:
25 min

Cooking time: 45 min

Serves 6

1½ pounds black cherries

5 eggs

½ cup superfine sugar, plus extra for dusting

4 tablespoons all-purpose flour

⅔ cup light cream

7 tablespoons milk

1 teaspoon grated lemon rind

1 tablespoon rum

1 tablespoon butter

salt

1. Preheat the oven to 350°F. Remove and discard the cherry stalks but leave the pits.

2. Whisk the eggs with the sugar and a pinch of salt. Add the flour and continue whisking while incorporating the cream and the milk.

3. Add the lemon rind and rum.

4. Butter a glazed shallow ovenproof dish and place the cherries in it in a closely packed layer. Pour the batter over them.

5. Bake the clafoutis for about 45 minutes, dotting the top with a few pats of butter halfway through the cooking time.

6. Dust the clafoutis with superfine sugar and leave to cool.

 TIP

YOU CAN ALSO MAKE individual clafoutis in small dishes. Use 10–12 cherries for each and pack them in the picnic basket still in their dishes. A variation replaces the cream and milk with 1 cup ricotta cheese.

TASTE BITE

THE MORE CHERRIES, the tastier the clafoutis. Cooking the cherries with the stones in gives them a delicious flavor, but don't forget to warn guests about the risk to their teeth!

Semolina cake with nectarines

Preparation time:
35 min

Cooking time: 45 min

Serves 6

4 nectarines

1¹/₂ cups sugar

generous 2 cups milk

3 cardamom seeds

1 cinnamon stick

**grated rind of
1 orange and
1 lemon**

¹/₂ cup fine semolina

2 tablespoons rum

2 eggs, beaten

1. Peel and pit the nectarines, then cut into small pieces. Dissolve ¹/₂ cup of the sugar in 1 cup water in a pan over low heat, then bring to a boil. Add the nectarines and simmer for 5 minutes. Drain and leave to cool.

2. Put ¹/₄ cup of the remaining sugar and ¹/₄ cup water in a flameproof flan dish and cook over high heat until it turns to a fairly dark caramel. Remove from the heat and tilt the dish until the sides are coated, then leave to cool.

3. Put the milk into a pan. Open the cardamoms and scrape the aromatic black seeds into the milk. Add the cinnamon stick and grated citrus rinds and bring to a boil.

4. Pour in the semolina, stirring constantly. Add the remaining sugar and cook for 2 minutes, stirring constantly, then add the rum.

5. Remove the semolina from the heat and leave to cool for 2 minutes. Remove the cinnamon stick and stir in the eggs and nectarines.

6. Preheat the oven to 350°F. Pour the prepared mixture into the caramel-coated dish and bake for 45 minutes. Leave to cool before turning the cake out of the dish.

TASTE BITE
THIS CAKE IS EXCELLENT served with a fresh fruit salad (nectarines, apricots, raspberries, melon) and small, crisp cookies.

Terrine of pork cooked in hard cider

Preparation time:
25 min, the day
before

Chilling: 12 hours

Cooking time:
3 hours

Serves 6

**leg of pork, about
3 pounds**

1 lemon

**3 tablespoons
peanut oil**

**2–3 onions, peeled
and sliced (about
12 ounces)**

**2 tablespoons wine
vinegar**

**scant 2 cups hard
cider**

**$\frac{1}{2}$ tablespoon
allspice**

2 cloves

**5–6 black
peppercorns**

2 bay leaves

**3 garlic cloves,
peeled**

**1 envelope
($\frac{1}{4}$ ounce) gelatin**

salt

1. Remove the skin from the pork and season the meat with salt.

2. Cut a thin layer of rind from the lemon and blanch it for 10 minutes in a pan of boiling water. Drain and reserve.

3. Heat the oil in a large, flameproof casserole. Add the pork and cook for 10 minutes, until browned on all sides, then remove, and set aside. Brown the onions in the same oil.

4. Preheat the oven to 300°F. Return the pork to the casserole and add the vinegar and all but $\frac{1}{4}$ cup of the hard cider. Add the spices, bay leaves, garlic, and lemon rind.

5. Cover and cook in the oven for about $2\frac{3}{4}$ hours (see TIP), then add the remaining hard cider.

6. Drain the meat, reserving the cooking liquid but discarding the spices and bay leaves. When the pork has cooled, remove the bone and cut the meat into small cubes.

7. Measure the reserved liquid into a pan and sprinkle over sufficient gelatin to set the quantity of liquid according to the packet instructions. Whisk over low heat to dissolve completely. Do not boil. Cool until beginning to thicken.

8. Stir in the meat cubes, onions, and garlic. Put into a terrine, cover with a piece of foil-wrapped cardboard and a weight. Chill for 12 hours.

TASTE BITE

EXCELLENT SLICED and served with onion relish or dill pickles. Leg of pork is also delicious cooked whole, then simply sliced when cold.

TIP

TO MAKE SURE THAT THE PORK is cooked through, turn it at regular intervals throughout the cooking period. It is done when the juices run clear after a knife point is inserted well into the meat.

a day
on the
river

Mussels, shrimp, and navy bean salad

Preparation time:
40 min,
overnight soaking

Cooking time:
1¾ hours

Serves 6

1½ cups dried navy beans, soaked overnight

2 onions, sliced

1 carrot, sliced

1 celery stalk, sliced

1 bouquet garni

1½ pounds fresh mussels

7 tablespoons dry white wine

1 large pink shallot

1 bunch flat leaf parsley

1 teaspoon apple vinegar

2 tablespoons olive oil

7 ounces small peeled, cooked shrimp

salt, pepper

1. Drain the beans, put them into a pan, and add cold water to cover. Add the onions, carrot, celery, and bouquet garni and bring to a boil. Boil rapidly for 10 minutes.

2. Lower the heat and simmer the beans for 1–1½ hours more, or until tender. They should be soft but not disintegrating. Discard the vegetables and bouquet garni and season the beans with salt and pepper.

3. Scrub the mussels under cold running water and pull off the beards. Discard any mussels with damaged shells or that do not shut immediately when sharply tapped. Put them into a pan with the white wine, cover tightly, and cook over high heat, shaking the pan occasionally. As soon as they open, remove from the heat and strain the cooking liquid into a bowl through a fine-mesh strainer. Shell the mussels, discarding any that remain shut.

4. For the vinaigrette, peel and chop the shallot and coarsely chop the parsley. Mash a few of the beans to a paste and stir this into the reserved cooking liquid. Add the vinegar, shallot, parsley and olive oil and season with salt and pepper. Coat the beans with this dressing, add the mussels and shrimp, place in an airtight container, and chill until needed.

TASTE BITE

DELICIOUS when the seasoning is just right. If the beans absorb some of the vinaigrette as they cool, don't hesitate to add extra salt and pepper and, perhaps, a dash of vinegar.

TIP

CANNED NAVY BEANS may be used instead of dried. This kind of salad also goes well with smoked fish.

Buckwheat wraps with salami

Preparation time: 10 min, the day before

Cooking time: 20 min

Serves 6

generous ³/₄ cup buckwheat flour

2 tablespoons olive oil

1 cup sparkling mineral water

1 tablespoon peanut oil

6 tablespoons butter

8 ounces salami, thinly sliced

salt, pepper

1. Prepare the dough for the wraps the previous day. Put the flour into a mixing bowl with a pinch of salt and pour in the oil and sparkling mineral water.

2. Mix together and knead until it is smooth, but do not let it become elastic. Set aside in the refrigerator.

3. The next day, divide the dough into six and roll out thin wraps. Heat a medium-size skillet and brush with oil. Cook the wraps, one at a time. Put a pat of butter about the size of a hazelnut on each one.

4. Remove any skin from around the edges of the salami. Put a layer of salami slices on the wraps, roll them up, and cut into rounds.

5. Secure with a toothpick to prevent them from unwinding and store in an airtight container until needed.

-☼- TIP

MAKE TWO OR THREE TIMES the amount if you intend serving these wraps with other dishes, such as cold meats or marinated fish (see Mackerel fillets with red currants on page 38), as part of the picnic.

Crab vinaigrette

Preparation time:
1 hour

Serves 4

6 cooked crabs

2 white shallots

2 tablespoons lemon juice

4 tablespoons mayonnaise

2 tablespoons chopped parsley

1 teaspoon chopped dill

cayenne pepper

dill pickles or mini-cucumbers

salt, pepper

1. Crack the large crab claws and the legs with nutcrackers and remove the meat.

2. Halve the body sections and pick out the white meat from the leg sockets. Scrape the dark meat from the shells, then select four shells for serving, and scrub them thoroughly. Check the claw meat carefully for pieces of shell, then set aside.

3. Peel and chop the shallots and combine with the crab meat in a bowl. Add the lemon juice, mayonnaise, parsley, and dill, season to taste with cayenne, salt, and pepper, cover, and keep cool.

4. Slice the dill pickles or cucumbers into rounds. To serve, fill the four prepared shells with the crab mixture and garnish with the dill pickles or cucumber slices.

 TIP

IF YOU LIKE, buy dressed crabs from a good fish store.

 TASTE BITE

SERVE with a tomato and cucumber salad.

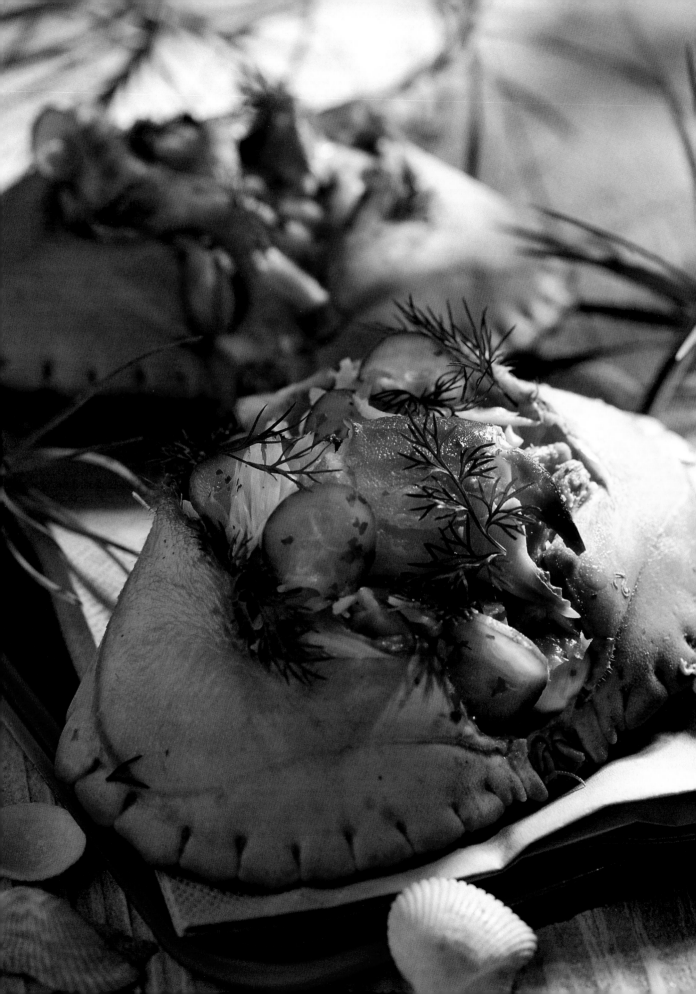

Jumbo shrimp with green mayonnaise

Preparation time: 30 min

Marinate: 2 hours

Cooking time: 35 min

Serves 6

TASTE BITE

EXCELLENT on buttered slices of rye bread with small boiled salad potatoes (see illustration).

TIP

THE GRAPESEED OIL stabilizes the mixture and prevents the mayonnaise from separating as a result of the warmth in the atmosphere. If using ready-made mayonnaise, add tarragon to it.

For the jumbo shrimp

24 jumbo shrimp

¹/₂ bottle dry white wine

1 celery stalk, chopped

1 tablespoon grated fresh ginger root

1 bay leaf

1 thyme sprig

juice of 1 lemon

salt, pepper

For the mayonnaise

1 egg yolk

scant 1 cup grapeseed oil

1 tablespoon chopped tarragon

1 tablespoon chopped parsley

1 tablespoon chopped chervil

salt, pepper

1. Pull off the heads and peel the shrimp, then remove the black intestinal thread along the back. Rinse and pat dry with paper towels.

2. Pour 3¾ cups water and the wine into a large pan and add the celery, ginger, bay leaf, thyme, and 2 tablespoons of the lemon juice. Bring to a boil and simmer for 30 minutes, then strain, and reserve the stock.

3. Bring the stock to a boil, lower the heat, add the shrimp, and boil gently for 5 minutes, or until cooked through. Drain and let cool.

4. To make the mayonnaise, put the egg yolk in a bowl, add a generous pinch of salt, and beat with a balloon whisk. When it begins to thicken, start adding the oil, a few drops at a time. If it remains liquid, continue whisking vigorously; the success of the mayonnaise depends on this early stage. Gradually drizzle in the oil until the mayonnaise has reached the required consistency. If it is too thick, add a little water and a dash of lemon juice to enhance the flavor.

5. Season with pepper, stir in the herbs, and set aside.

6. Pack the shrimp in a separate container from the mayonnaise. Serve on slices of bread with salad.

Sardines in a spicy sauce with bread and red butter

Preparation time:
30 min

Marinate: 4 hours

Cooking time: 15 min

Serves 6

12 fresh sardines

5 tablespoons olive oil

2 shallots, peeled and chopped

2 garlic cloves, peeled and chopped

¹/₂ chilli pepper

²/₃ cup white wine

²/₃ cup apple vinegar

1 bay leaf

2 teaspoons coriander seeds

For the red butter

1 tablespoon paprika

pinch cayenne pepper

¹/₂ cup butter, softened

4 tablespoons lemon juice

1 shallot, peeled and chopped

salt

1. Scale and rinse the sardines, dry on paper towels, and remove the heads.

2. Open the fish and detach the fillets from the backbone, rinse them, and pat dry with paper towels.

3. Heat the olive oil in a skillet and add the sardines, skin side down, and seal for 30 seconds. Remove from the heat and leave the oil in the pan.

4. Arrange the sardines, head to tail, in an earthenware dish.

5. Cook the shallots and garlic gently in the oil remaining in the skillet. Add the chilli pepper, white wine, vinegar, bay leaf, and coriander seeds, bring to a boil, and boil vigorously to reduce by one-fourth. Let cool for 1 minute, then pour the mixture over the sardines. Leave in a cool place for 4 hours.

6. For the red butter, beat the paprika and cayenne pepper into the softened butter, gradually adding the lemon juice. Add the chopped shallot and a pinch of salt. Put the butter mixture into a pot and store in a cool place. Serve the sardines on slices of bread spread with the red butter.

☀ TIP

FOR SOMETHING in a similar vein, take a can of sardines in olive oil and mash with some butter, add a few drops of lemon juice, a pinch of cayenne pepper, and a little chopped shallot. While not very pretty, this "pâté" is absolutely delicious spread on crusty bread. Make a little pot of it especially for those who are hooked on the flavor.

Potato and taramasalata pancakes

Preparation time:
35 min

Cooking time: 35 min

Serves 6

**For the
taramasalata**

**5 ounces smoked
cod roe**

**2 tablespoons lemon
juice**

**handful stale white
bread crumbs**

1 cup sour cream

grapeseed oil

salt, pepper

For the pancakes

**10 ounces salad
potatoes, peeled**

1 zucchini, grated

**3 tablespoons all-
purpose flour**

**3 tablespoons sour
cream**

3 eggs

pinch grated nutmeg

1. To prepare the taramasalata, remove the fine membrane from the cod roes and put them into a food processor, together with the lemon juice, bread crumbs, and sour cream and process until thoroughly combined. Alternatively, beat them together with a balloon whisk in a bowl.

2. With the processor running, gradually add the oil until a creamy consistency is reached. Season to taste and set aside.

3. To prepare the pancakes, cook the potatoes for 15 minutes in boiling water. Add the grated zucchini and cook for 5 minutes more, then drain.

4. While the potatoes and zucchini are still hot, mash them with a fork. Stir in the flour and sour cream and add the eggs, one at a time, but take care not to overmix. Season with the nutmeg.

5. Heat a large, nonstick skillet. Drop spoonfuls of the mixture into the skillet and cook until golden underneath. Flip over with a metal spatula and cook the other side. Place them in an airtight container, when cold, and serve them with the taramasalata.

TIP

TARAMASALATA made with smoked cod roe is very pale pink because it contains no artificial coloring matter.

TASTE BITE

GOOD WITH A SQUEEZE OF LEMON. Stack the pancakes after the style of a club sandwich, adding slices of smoked salmon, dill sprigs, and thin slices of cucumber.

Mackerel fillets with red currants

Preparation time:
25 min

Marinate: 1 hour

Cooking time:
30 min

Serves 6

3 mackerel, each weighing about 12 ounces, filleted or 6 pre-packed fillets

1³/₄ cups red currants

1 tablespoon balsamic vinegar

1 tablespoon grated fresh ginger root

1 tablespoon soy sauce

1 tablespoon olive oil

1 onion

3–4 pieces of sun-dried tomato in olive oil, drained and finely chopped

6 unsweetened crêpes or tortilla wraps

pepper

1. Place the mackerel fillets in a nonmetallic dish, skin side down.

2. Squeeze the juice from 1 cup of the red currants by crushing them by hand. Keep the rest of the currants to garnish the fish fillets.

3. Add the balsamic vinegar, grated ginger, and soy sauce to the red currant juice.

4. Pour this over the fish fillets and marinate for 1 hour in a cool place.

5. Drain and reserve the marinade. Pat the fillets dry with paper towels and slice into 1-inch wide strips.

6. Heat the oil in a skillet and add the mackerel strips, cut side down, and cook for a few seconds, then sprinkle with a little salt and season with pepper. Pour in the marinade and cook for a few more seconds, then remove from the heat.

7. Pack the fillets into a container with the onion, cut in rings, and the pieces of sun-dried tomato. To serve, wrap the mixture in the crêpes or wraps and garnish with the reserved red currants.

TIP

IF SERVING these as part of an outdoor meal, they could be presented in the form of mini-pizzas. Cut six rounds of puff pastry and spread with tomato pizza sauce and pieces of raw mackerel. Bake in a very hot oven for about 3 minutes.

Brittany plum and apple dessert

Preparation time:
20 min

Cooking time: 45 min

Serves 6

4 eggs

¹/₂ cup superfine sugar

1³/₄ cups all-purpose flour

1 cup butter, melted

2 tablespoons rum

1³/₄ cups whole milk

2 eating apples, peeled and grated

13 ounces purple plums, halved and pitted

1. Preheat the oven to 400°F. Whisk the eggs and sugar together until pale and fluffy.

2. Continue whisking, gradually adding the flour. Continue to whisk to prevent lumps from forming. Add the melted butter and the rum.

3. Gradually add the milk, whisking constantly, to make a thin batter.

4. Add the grated apple and plum halves to the batter.

5. Pour the mixture into a buttered oven dish and bake for 35 minutes, then increase the temperature to 425°F and cook for 10 minutes more to brown the top, but check after 5 minutes to make sure it is not over-browning.

 TIP

THE APPLES give a touch of acidity and improve the appearance of the dessert.

 TASTE BITE

VERY GOOD with straw-berries or an assortment of fruit, such as apples, peaches, and strawberries, threaded on skewers with mint leaves.

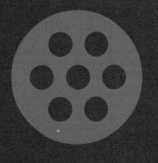

out of
town

Club sandwich
(Salmon, avocados, shrimp, Cheddar cheese)

Preparation time:
30 min

Serves 6

12 slices white bread

12 slices whole-wheat bread

2 avocados

4 tablespoons lemon juice

1/4 cup cream cheese

4 ounces smoked salmon

6 dill sprigs

5 ounces cooked, peeled shrimp

1 bunch chervil

6 lettuce leaves

6 teaspoons plum chutney

12 thin slices Cheddar cheese

salt, pepper

skewers

 TIP

A LITTLE BUTTER spread on the bread prevents it from drying out. If plum chutney is not available, substitute plum jam and sharpen it with a slight dash of vinegar.

1. Toast the white and whole-wheat bread slices on both sides.

2. Peel, pit, and slice the avocados, and sprinkle with lemon juice to prevent them from discoloring. Season with salt and pepper.

3. Assemble the sandwiches, alternating whole-wheat and white bread and using four slices per sandwich. Put a little cream cheese with the smoked salmon; a squeeze of lemon and a few dill sprigs with the shrimp; sprigs of chervil, avocado slices, lettuce, and plum chutney with the Cheddar.

4. Stack the sandwiches in a pile and cut them in half diagonally. Secure with a skewer through the center, wrap them in foil, and store in an airtight container until required.

Haddock and herring snack

Preparation time:
15 min

Cooking time: 20 min

Serves 6

**12 small salad
potatoes**

**10 ounces undyed
smoked haddock
fillets with skin**

**4 sweet-cured
herrings**

**3¹/₂ tablespoons
white wine**

**1 tablespoon
sherry vinegar**

**3 tablespoons
peanut oil**

**2 white onions,
peeled and finely
chopped**

**1 teaspoon grated
fresh ginger root**

**2 tablespoons
chopped chives**

salt, pepper

1. Cook the potatoes in their skins for 10–15 minutes in lightly salted, boiling water.

2. Place the haddock flat and with a knife blade held at an angle, cut into very thin slices. Cut the herring slices into four.

3. Drain the potatoes, peel them, and cut into rounds. Make a dressing by combining the white wine, sherry vinegar, and oil and mix well with the potatoes and chopped onion.

4. Add the fish to the potato salad, together with the ginger and chives. Season with pepper and keep in a cool place.

 TASTE BITE

GOOD as a filling for little toasted sesame seed rolls.

TIP

IN THIS DISH the haddock is left raw. If, however, you should find it too salty (this is governed by the quality of the fish) marinate it for 1 hour before use in a little lemon juice or white wine.

Cold lamb and mint sauce on an open sandwich

Preparation time:
25 min

Cooking time: 30 min

Serves 6

1 tablespoon butter

1 tablespoon ras-el-hanout

1¹/₂ pounds leg of lamb, boned and rolled

1 bunch mint

scant 1 cup sour cream

1 loaf coarse country bread

1 handful young spinach leaves

sea salt

salt, pepper

1. Preheat the oven to 400°F.

2. Melt the butter and combine with the ras-al-hanout, and season with salt and pepper. Coat the lamb all over with this flavored butter.

3. Brown the meat on all sides in a skillet, then put it into a roasting pan, and baste with any remaining flavored butter. Roast for 25–30 minutes, then leave to cool for 15 minutes. If the meat is to be well done, make sure the juices run clear when the point of a knife is inserted.

4. Finely chop the mint leaves and season with salt and pepper, then add the sour cream. Slice the bread and toast it on both sides. Wash the spinach and pat dry with paper towels.

5. Carve the cold lamb and lay slices on the toast. Garnish with the spinach leaves and serve it with the mint sauce and a sprinkling of sea salt.

(Ras-el-hanout is an exotic and complex blend of numerous spices, including cloves, cinnamon, nutmeg, cardamom and peppercorns, used in Moroccan and Tunisian cuisine. Look for it in delicatessens and Middle Eastern specialty stores.)

Stilton and Cheddar terrine with bacon

Preparation time:
25 min

Chilling: 2 hours

Serves 6

7 ounces Stilton cheese

scant $^{1}/_{2}$ cup butter

2 tablespoons brandy

5 ounces Cheddar cheese

2 tablespoons sour cream

$^{1}/_{2}$ cup shelled pistachio nuts

8 bacon strips, lightly broiled

pepper

1. Mash the Stilton and butter together with a fork to make a smooth paste, mixing in brandy to taste and a little black pepper.

2. Cut the Cheddar into pieces and put in a food processor with 1 tablespoon sour cream. Process thoroughly to a smooth paste, adding a little more sour cream if necessary.

3. Coarsely chop the pistachios in the food processor. Line a rectangular terrine or loaf pan with plastic wrap and spread a layer of creamed Stilton over the base. Cover with strips of bacon and some of the chopped pistachios. Add a layer of creamed Cheddar, then more bacon and nuts. Continue with the layers until all the ingredients are used up. Cover with foil-wrapped cardboard and a weight. Chill for 2 hours before using.

TASTE BITE
SLICE AND SERVE with poppy seed rolls.

TIP
STILTON is a medium blue-veined cheese with a crusty rind and a very pronounced flavor. Cheddar is a pressed cheese with a natural rind. Avoid the factory-made varieties if possible.

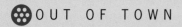

Chicken pie

Preparation time:
45 min

Cooking time: 1 hour

Serves 6

¹/₄ cup butter

1 pound diced lean
pork

1¹/₄ pounds chicken
thighs

4 onions, peeled
and sliced

3¹/₄ cups chopped
white mushrooms

1¹/₄ cups sherry

pinch tandoori
spice

pinch apple pie
spice

2 pounds green
asparagus

shortcrust pie
dough, rolled into
2 rounds to fit the
pie pan

salt

*Note: If you like, use half
pork and half veal*

1. Melt half the butter in a large skillet and gently cook the diced pork for 5 minutes, then transfer to a flameproof casserole. Add the chicken to the skillet and cook for 10 minutes, adding the onions halfway.

2. Transfer the chicken and onions to the casserole. Add the mushrooms and the remaining butter to the skillet and cook for 2 minutes, then transfer them to the casserole.

3. Stir 1 cup of the sherry into the skillet, then pour it over the meat. Add the spices, cover, and cook on the stovetop for 20 minutes.

4. Cut off the tough stems of the asparagus and cook the tips for 10 minutes in lightly salted, boiling water, then drain.

5. Remove the meat from the casserole. Remove and discard the chicken skin and bones and cut the flesh into cubes.

6. Process the pork, mushrooms, and cooking liquid in a food processor, then transfer to a bowl. Stir in the chicken, asparagus, and remaining sherry.

7. Preheat the oven to 400°F. Line a nonstick pie pan with one round of dough. Pile on the prepared mixture, cover with the second round of dough, and seal the edges. Make a couple of cuts in the lid to let the steam escape. Bake for 30 minutes.

Apple crisp with mango

Preparation time:
25 min, 1 hour in
advance

Cooking time: 40 min

Serves 6

$\frac{1}{2}$ cup raisins

2 tablespoons rum

**1 cup all-purpose
flour**

**scant $\frac{1}{2}$ cup brown
sugar**

**$\frac{2}{3}$ cup softened
butter**

6 eating apples

1 ripe mango

1 cinnamon stick

salt

1. Place the raisins in a small bowl, add the rum, and let soak until plump.

2. Put the flour, a pinch of salt, and $\frac{1}{3}$ cup of the brown sugar in a mixing bowl. Rub in $\frac{1}{2}$ cup butter with your fingertips to the consistency of coarse bread crumbs and chill for 1 hour.

3. Peel and core the apples. Peel the mango and remove the pit. Cut the fruit into pieces.

4. Cook the fruit for 15–20 minutes in a large skillet with 2 tablespoons of butter, the remaining brown sugar, and the cinnamon stick. Stir frequently until the apples are mushy and the juice that ran from the mango has evaporated. Add the drained raisins.

5. Preheat the oven to 425°F. Lightly butter an ovenproof dish.

6. Remove and discard the cinnamon stick and arrange the fruit in the dish. Spread the topping over it. Bake for 20 minutes, until the crust is golden and crisp.

TASTE BITE
GOOD served with whipped cream—remember to pack a spray can of whipped cream in the hamper.

TIP
THE EASIEST METHOD of carrying the crisp to the picnic is to leave it in the dish. One lucky person gets to scrape out the crusty bits left in the dish.

Cake flavored with citrus rind

Preparation time:
25 min

Soaking time: 1 hour

Cooking time: 45 min

Serves 6

generous ¹/₂ cup lemon and candied orange rind

3 tablespoons rum

1³/₄ cups all-purpose flour

1 teaspoon baking powder

²/₃ cup softened butter

¹/₂ cup superfine sugar

3 eggs

salt

1. Cut up the citrus rinds with scissors and put them into a bowl. Add the rum and let soak for 1 hour.

2. Preheat the oven to 350°F. Sift the flour with the baking powder and a pinch of salt into a bowl. Beat the butter and sugar together to a creamy consistency in another bowl. Beat in the eggs, one at a time, then the flour. When the mixture is smooth, add the rinds and rum.

3. Pour the mixture into a nonstick cake pan and bake for 45 minutes. When the top has risen, increase the oven temperature to 400°F to finish browning the cake, but take care it doesn't burn.

TASTE BITE
SERVE WARM OR COLD with tea laced with a little whiskey, brought along in a vacuum flask.

TIP
RAISINS SOAKED in rum could be substituted for the citrus rind.

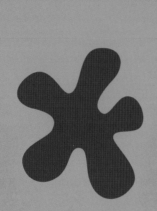

beaches
and sand
dunes

Eggplant, ricotta cheese, and prosciutto rolls

Preparation time: 25 min

Cooking time: 40 min

Serves 6

6 small eggplant

1 chopped garlic clove

¹/₂ cup olive oil

1¹/₄ cups ricotta cheese

1 tablespoon balsamic vinegar

1 tablespoon chopped mint

1 tablespoon chopped parsley

1 tablespoon chopped basil, plus extra leaves

6 tomatoes

6 small ciabatta loaves, or any large crusty rolls

1 sun-dried tomato in olive oil, drained and finely chopped

6 slices prosciutto

salt, pepper

1. Preheat the oven to 400°F. Make an incision around the stem end of the eggplant, place them on the center oven shelf, and cook for 40 minutes, until the skins are shriveled. Leave them to cool, then cut in half, scoop out the pulp, and season with salt and pepper.

2. Add the chopped garlic to the eggplant pulp and whisk the mixture while gradually adding 4–6 tablespoons of the olive oil to obtain a creamy consistency. Set aside in a cool place.

3. Mash the ricotta with a fork. Add the balsamic vinegar and 2 tablespoons of olive oil. Season with salt and pepper.

4. Stir the chopped mint, parsley, and basil into the ricotta cheese.

5. Halve the tomatoes, remove the cores and seeds, and dice the flesh.

6. Split the loaves or rolls in half and spread with the fillings, combining half the ricotta with the sun-dried tomato; the remaining ricotta with slices of prosciutto; and the eggplant with the diced fresh tomatoes and the whole basil leaves torn into strips.

-⊙- TIP

FOCACCIA or any other flatbread can also be used.

Egg-filled rolls

Preparation time:
25 min

Serves 6

2 small green bell
peppers

4 tomatoes

3 hard-cooked eggs

bunch of scallions

1 large garlic clove

6 round, flat bread
rolls

1 teaspoon vinegar

3 tablespoons olive
oil

3¹/₂ ounces assorted
salad greens
(arugula, frisée
lettuce, chervil)

12 canned anchovy
fillets, drained

24 pitted black
olives

2 basil sprigs

salt, pepper

TIP

A MORE LUXURIOUS SNACK
can be made by spreading
tapenade (see page 125) on
the bread and garnishing
with marinated raw fish
fillets, such as sardines and
Mackerel fillets with red
currants (see page 38), or
even with sliced salami.

1. Char the skins of the bell peppers until they blister, either over a gas flame or under a hot broiler. Put in a plastic bag for 5 minutes to loosen the skins, and then peel and slice them.

2. Slice the tomatoes; shell the hard-cooked eggs, and slice into rounds. Slice the scallions and peel the garlic.

3. Split the bread rolls in half and discard some of the soft crumb. Rub the inside surfaces with the garlic.

4. Combine the vinegar and olive oil and season with salt and pepper. Sprinkle a few drops over the insides of the rolls. Arrange the salad greens, scallions, bell peppers, tomatoes, and egg slices on the bases. Top with the anchovies, olives, and torn basil leaves. Sprinkle on the remaining oil and vinegar dressing.

5. Cover with the top halves of the rolls and wrap in plastic wrap.

Catalan-style bread with marinated sea bass

Preparation time:
30 min

Marinate: 1 hour

Serves 6

1–1¼ pounds sea bass fillet

1 lime

3 scallions

1 chilli pepper

2 fennel or dill sprigs, coarsely chopped

3 ripe tomatoes

12 large slices coarse country bread

olive oil

salt, pepper

1. For the marinade, cut the sea bass into strips and place in a nonmetallic dish, squeeze the juice from the lime, and chop the scallions. Seed the chilli pepper and cut into rings.

2. Sprinkle the lime juice, chilli pepper, scallions, and fennel or dill over the fish. Cover with plastic wrap and set aside for 1 hour in a cool place.

3. Cut a tomato in half and rub it over the slices of bread so that the pulp seeps in. Season with salt and pepper and a drizzle of olive oil. Slice the remaining tomatoes.

4. Drain the fish and season it with salt and several twists of the pepper mill.

5. Arrange the strips of sea bass on the bread slices, alternating with tomato slices.

◎ TASTE BITE

IF YOU LEAVE the preparation of the bread until the last minute, you will be rewarded with the fruity aromas of the tomato pulp and the olive oil.

 TIP

THIS RECIPE is based on *ceviche*—the South American dish of raw fish marinated in citrus juice, usually lime. Porgy or tuna can replace the sea bass. Whatever kind of fish is used, it must be really super-fresh.

Olive and thyme bread

Preparation time:
25 min, 1 hour
in advance

Cooking time: 55 min

Serves 6–8

For the dough

**1¹⁄₂ ounces fresh yeast
(if using dried yeast, follow the packet instructions and see TIP)**

4 cups all-purpose flour

2 teaspoons superfine sugar

1 teaspoon salt

4 tablespoons olive oil

For the topping

3¹⁄₂ tablespoons olive oil

3 pounds onions, finely chopped

1 teaspoon sugar

2 thyme sprigs

16 canned anchovies in oil (optional)

16 pitted black olives

salt, pepper

1. First, make the bread dough. In a small bowl, stir the yeast into 1¹⁄₄ cups lukewarm water. Sift the flour with the sugar and salt into a mixing bowl and make a well in the center.

2. Pour the olive oil and the dissolved yeast into the well and incorporate the flour by hand, kneading the dough until it forms a smooth ball. Leave to rest for 1 hour in a cool place.

3. For the topping, heat the oil in a heavy pan. Add the onions, cover, and cook over low heat for 30 minutes, until all the liquid has evaporated.

4. Sprinkle the onions with the sugar, season with salt, and cook gently, uncovered, for about 10 minutes to color slightly. Rub the thyme and add the leaves to the onion.

5. Preheat the oven to 400°F. Oil a cookie sheet or pizza pan. Flour the counter and roll out the dough to a thickness of ¹⁄₄ inch.

6. Place the dough on the cookie sheet and make a rim. Leave to rise for 15 minutes at room temperature, then top with the onions, anchovy fillets, and black olives. Bake for 15–20 minutes, until the edges are browned.

TIP

IF YOU USE dried yeast in place of fresh yeast, leave the dough to rise for longer than indicated on the packet. You could also make this dish with a ready-prepared pizza base.

Red snapper and bell pepper flan

Preparation time:
35 min

Cooking time: 30 min

Serves 6

**6 red snapper,
filleted**

**3 tablespoons olive
oil**

**2 red onions,
chopped**

**3 small yellow bell
peppers**

1 garlic clove

1 tablespoon butter

**10 ounces puff
pastry dough,
thawed if frozen**

**1 tablespoon
chopped chives**

sea salt, pepper

1. Check the fish fillets for any bones that have been overlooked, then place the fish in a cool place.

2. Heat 2 tablespoons of the oil in a skillet, add the onions, and cook over low heat for 20 minutes. Remove from the heat and set aside to cool.

3. Char the bell peppers over a gas flame or under a hot broiler, then place in a plastic bag for 5 minutes to let the steam loosen the skins. Peel and crush the garlic.

4. Peel and seed the bell peppers. Cut the flesh into strips and put in a dish with the garlic and the remaining oil.

5. Preheat the oven to 400°F. Grease a cookie sheet. Roll out the dough into a rectangle about 16 x 6 inches and place on the cookie sheet. Make a rim all around it.

6. Cut the fish into strips. Cover the pastry with the onion, the strips of fish, and bell peppers, reserving two or three strips of bell pepper for the garnish. Bake for 10 minutes.

7. Chop the reserved strips of bell pepper into small dice and sprinkle over the flan with the chives. Season with sea salt and pepper.

-ᗝ- TIP

FROZEN FISH FILLETS can
be used equally well for this
delicious dish.

Assortment of crudités with anchovy, tuna, goat cheese, and shrimp dips

Preparation time:
1 hour

Serves 6

For the raw vegetables

carrots, black radishes, tomatoes, fennel, small artichokes, white mushrooms, celery, scallions, cucumber, red, yellow, and green bell peppers

For the shrimp dip
3½ ounces cooked, peeled shrimp

scant ½ cup cottage cheese

7 tablespoons sour cream

2 tablespoons lemon juice

1 tablespoon tomato ketchup

1 teaspoon soy sauce

3 tablespoons olive oil

½ garlic clove

salt, pepper

For the anchovy dip

12 canned anchovy fillets in olive oil

4 garlic cloves

2 tablespoons lemon juice

2 tablespoons olive oil

pepper

For the tuna dip

5 ounces canned tuna in olive oil

4 tablespoons capers

2 tablespoons lemon juice

scant 1 cup cottage cheese

1 tablespoon coarsely chopped parsley and chives

1 teaspoon curry powder

salt, pepper

For the goat cheese dip

2 small round goat cheeses

scant 1 cup cottage cheese

1 teaspoon balsamic vinegar

1 tablespoon chopped basil

salt, pepper

1. Scrape the carrots, cut them lengthwise into sticks, and cover with plastic wrap.

2. Trim the roots from the radishes. Leave the other vegetables whole.

3. Prepare the dips as described below and store in jars.

4. For the shrimp dip, process all the ingredients to a creamy consistency in a food processor blender. Season with salt and pepper.

5. For the anchovy dip, drain the anchovies, and process them with the garlic, 1 teaspoon water, and the lemon juice in a food processor. With the motor running, gradually add the olive oil, a little at a time, until combined. Season with pepper.

6. For the tuna dip, drain the fish and process it in a food processor with the capers and lemon juice. Alternatively, mash it with a fork. Stir in the cottage cheese, herbs, and curry powder. Season with salt and pepper.

7. For the goat cheese dip, process the goat cheese with the cottage cheese and balsamic vinegar in a food processor, or mash with a fork. Add the basil, mix well, and season with salt and pepper.

Terrine Niçoise

Preparation time: 25 min

Cooking time: 30 min

Serves 6

10 ounces salad potatoes, peeled

6 tablespoons butter

1¹/₂ cups fine green beans

6 quail eggs or 3 hard-cooked hen's eggs, halved

14-ounce can tuna in brine

²/₃ cup plain yogurt

2 tablespoons lemon juice

8 basil leaves, torn into pieces

salt, pepper

1. Cook the potatoes in lightly salted, boiling water for 20 minutes, then drain, add the butter, and mash with a fork.

2. Trim the green beans and cook in lightly salted, boiling water for 6–8 minutes, until tender-crisp. Drain thoroughly and set aside.

3. Boil the quail eggs, if using, for 3 minutes, then cool under cold running water before shelling.

4. Drain the tuna and stir it into the mashed potato, add the yogurt, and mix thoroughly to a smooth paste. Add the lemon juice and basil and season with salt and pepper.

5. Line a terrine or a rectangular mold with plastic wrap. Make a layer of beans in the base and pour half the tuna mixture over them. Place the quail eggs or halved hen's eggs in a single line down the center, pressing them in slightly. Cover with the remaining tuna mixture and top with the beans.

6. Cover with foil-wrapped cardboard and a weight. Store in the refrigerator until required.

TASTE BITE
SERVE WITH CHERRY TOMATOES and either tapenade (see page 125) or mayonnaise.

TIP
THE PLASTIC WRAP LINING makes it easier to turn the terrine out of the mold. Alternatively, you could serve the terrine directly from the mold.

Eggplant and zucchini carpaccio with mozzarella cheese

Preparation time:
30 min, 3 hours
before

Cooking time: 10 min

Serves 6

3 small eggplant

3 small zucchini

olive oil

1 tablespoon chopped basil

1 tablespoon chopped parsley

2 garlic cloves, peeled and chopped

3 mozzarella cheeses, each 4 ounces

coarse salt, pepper

1. Cut the eggplant lengthwise into slices about $\frac{1}{8}$ inch thick. Layer them in a strainer with a sprinkling of coarse salt between the layers and let stand for 2 hours. Prepare the zucchini in the same way but stand for only 1 hour.

2. Preheat the broiler. Rinse the eggplant and zucchini slices and pat them dry on paper towels. Arrange the slices on a broiler pan and broil briefly, then quickly turn the slices over. Transfer to a dish, drizzle a little olive oil over them, sprinkle with the chopped herbs and garlic, and leave to marinate for 1 hour.

3. Cut the mozzarella cheeses into pieces. Roll a strip of eggplant or zucchini around each and secure in place with a toothpick.

TASTE BITE
EXCELLENT with sliced ham, toast, and anchovy fillets marinated in olive oil.

TIP
OTHER VEGETABLES, such as red, yellow and green bell peppers, tomatoes, and fennel all go well with mozzarella cheese. Those that are unsuitable for the wrapping technique can simply be topped with a round of cheese.

Pine nut tart

Preparation time:
30 min

Cooking time: 35 min

Serves 6

For the dough

2 cups all-purpose flour

1 tablespoon superfine sugar

1 egg

1/₂ cup butter

salt

For the filling

2 tablespoons raisins

2 tablespoons rum

scant 1/₂ cup softened butter

1/₄ cup superfine sugar

2 eggs

1/₂ cup ground almonds

scant 1 cup pine nuts

 TASTE BITE

THIS TART is particularly delicious with apricot or plum compote.

1. For the dough, sift the flour into a large bowl, make a well in the center, and place the sugar, a pinch of salt, and the egg in it.

2. Dice the butter, add to the well, and mix together rapidly by hand. Roll the pastry into a ball, wrap it in a floured dishtowel, and let rest for 2 hours in a cool place.

3. For the filling: put the raisins in a bowl with the rum and let soak. Beat the butter and sugar together in a bowl. Beat the eggs together with the ground almonds in another bowl. Gradually add the butter and sugar mixture. Drain the raisins, stir them into the mixture, then mix in 3/4 cup of the pine nuts. Set aside.

4. Preheat the oven to 400°F. Lightly flour the counter and roll out the dough. Line a quiche pan with it and crimp the rim. Spoon in the pine nut mixture, spreading it evenly, and sprinkle the remaining pine nuts on the top. Bake for 35 minutes, or until the top is firm and golden brown.

Corsican cheesecake (Fiadone)

Preparation time:
20 min

Cooking time: 1 hour

Serves 6

**3 cups ricotta
cheese**

5 eggs, separated

**scant 1 cup
superfine sugar**

**grated rind of
1 lemon**

peanut oil

salt

1. Preheat the oven to 325°F. Grease and flour a 9-inch springform cake pan.

2. Cream the ricotta until smooth with an electric mixer, or by rubbing through a strainer. Whisk the egg yolks with the sugar in a mixing bowl until pale, thickened, and creamy.

3. Gradually add the ricotta to the egg and sugar mixture, together with the lemon rind. Add a pinch of salt to the egg whites in another bowl and whisk until stiff, then fold gently into the egg yolk mixture. Make sure the mixture is fully blended, but take care not to overmix or knock out the air.

4. Pour into the cake pan and smooth the top with a wet spatula. Bake for about 1 hour, or until the top is golden brown and the cheesecake has shrunk away from the sides of the pan. Turn out onto a wire rack to cool.

TASTE BITE

EXCELLENT eaten warm the same day or cold the following day, with a fruit salad or a fruit compote made with apricots, peaches, and almonds, accompanied by a sweet dessert wine.

Fresh goat cheese with figs

Preparation time:
25 min, 2 hours
in advance

Serves 6

6 basil sprigs

**14 ounces fresh
goat cheese**

**³/₄ cup whole
blanched almonds**

**14 ounces fresh
purple figs**

salt, pepper

1. Preheat the oven to 350°F. Coarsely chop the basil leaves. Process the goat cheese in a food processor until smooth or press through a strainer. Season with salt and pepper and add the basil.

2. Coarsely chop the almonds and toast in the oven or under the broiler until golden brown. Set aside. Watch them carefully, as the almonds can burn easily. Remove the stalks from the figs.

3. Roll the figs in the cheese until they are completely coated, then press in the chopped almonds all over the cheese surface. Let stand for 2 hours in a cool place.

4. To serve, cut each fig in half to display the fruit in the center.

 TIP

THIS CHEESE MIXTURE can be used to coat large grapes. Pistachio nuts may be used in place of the almonds. Choose cheeses that are not too moist or the mixture will be too sticky to handle.

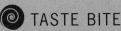 TASTE BITE

VERY GOOD with walnut bread, wholegrain bread, or poppy or sesame seed rolls, accompanied by a fruity white wine.

beneath
the pines

Pimiento boats with lightly salted cod filling

Preparation time:
35 min, 2 hours in
advance

Cooking time: 20 min

Serves 6

12 ounces cod fillet

sea salt

**18 mild green
pimientos or
9 green bell
peppers, halved
and seeded**

**2 salad potatoes,
peeled**

**1 garlic clove,
peeled**

**7 tablespoons sour
cream**

olive oil

**1 tablespoon
chopped chives**

curry powder

salt, pepper

1. Sprinkle the cod liberally with sea salt and leave in a cool place.

2. Hold the pimientos, if using, in a gas flame or place under a hot broiler for 2 minutes to blister the skin. Put in a plastic bag, tie the top, and leave for 10 minutes before peeling.

3. Slit the pimientos lengthwise and remove the membranes and seeds. Cook the potatoes in a small pan of lightly salted, boiling water for about 20 minutes, or until soft.

4. Rinse the cod under cold running water and place in a pan. Add water to cover. Bring to a gentle simmer, then turn off the heat, and let the fish poach in the hot water for 5 minutes.

5. Process the fish with the garlic in a food processor. Mash the potatoes and combine with the fish, then add the sour cream and enough olive oil to make the mixture creamy. Stir in the chopped chives.

6. Fill the pimiento or bell pepper halves with the fish mixture and lightly dust with curry powder.

TASTE BITE

SERVE WITH CROUTONS rubbed with garlic and olive oil for extra flavor.

TIP

DELICATE PIMIENTOS, in season around mid-August, are quickly past their best and need preparing as soon as possible after purchase. This dish can also be made with red bell peppers.

Tuna à la tartare with mustard seeds

Preparation time: 20 min

Marinate: 1 hour

Serves 6

1¼ pounds fresh tuna fillet

2 teaspoons hot mustard

3 tablespoons olive oil

¼ teaspoon grated lemon rind

1 bunch chives, coarsely chopped

1 bunch dill, coarsely chopped

2 teaspoons mustard seeds

½ teaspoon salt

1 teaspoon coarsely ground coriander seeds

lemon juice

sea salt, pepper

1. Lay the tuna flat on a board and cut into thin strips, then into cubes.

2. Combine the mustard with the olive oil in a bowl. Add the diced tuna, grated lemon rind, and 4 tablespoons of the chopped herbs. Season with pepper and mix well, then add the mustard seeds, salt, and coriander seeds. Stir thoroughly.

3. Cover and set aside in a cool place for 1 hour. Sprinkle with lemon juice before serving.

TASTE BITE

SERVE ON SLICES OF BREAD accompanied by crudités (see Assortment of crudités with their dips, page 66).

TIP

CHOOSE A PIECE OF TUNA from the thick part of the back, so that you can slice it along the grain of the meat.

Cold patties with gazpacho sauce

Preparation time:
40 min

Cooking time: 30 min

Serves 6

For the patties

1 thick slice ham or prosciutto with its fat

7 ounces bulk sausage

¹/₂ onion

3 garlic cloves

1 bunch parsley

3-4 eggs

5 handfuls stale white bread, made into crumbs

3 tablespoons peanut oil

1 pound bottled strained tomatoes

sea salt, pepper

For the gazpacho sauce

1¹/₂ pounds tomatoes

2 onions

1 cucumber

2 red bell peppers

1 garlic clove

1 tablespoon wine vinegar

2 tablespoons olive oil

1 green bell pepper

salt, pepper

1. For the patties, remove the rind from the ham or prosciutto, if necessary; coarsely chop, and mix into the bulk sausage. Finely chop the onion, garlic, and parsley.

2. Combine the meat mixture with 3 eggs, the onion, garlic, parsley, and the bread crumbs; season with salt and pepper, and mix well. The resulting mixture should be quite soft. Add another egg yolk if necessary.

3. Heat the peanut oil in a skillet and drop in spoonfuls of the mixture, flattening them to form round patties. Brown the patties on both sides and drain on paper towels.

4. Heat the bottled strained tomatoes in a pan, add the patties, and cook for 30 minutes over low heat. Remove the patties and drain. Transfer the cooking liquid to a food processor.

5. For the gazpacho sauce, peel and seed the tomatoes and chop the flesh. Coarsely chop the onions, a fourth of the cucumber, and 1 seeded red bell pepper. Crush the garlic. Add all these ingredients to the cooking liquid in the food processor, together with the wine vinegar and olive oil. Blend to a creamy consistency, season, and chill in the refrigerator for 3 hours.

6. Prepare the rest of the vegetables to make crudités and serve them with the patties and the gazpacho sauce.

TASTE BITE

THE PATTIES will be all the better if prepared the day before. The gazpacho, with ice cubes added to chill and dilute it, can also be served as a soup. Pack it in an insulated container.

Squid stuffed with herbs

Preparation time:
45 min

Cooking time:
35–40 min

Serves 6

6 squid

1 shallot

1 garlic clove

1 small bunch each chives, basil, and parsley

6 slices coarse country bread

1 tablespoon olive oil

1 egg

12 ounces bottled strained tomatoes

2 tablespoons brandy

1 bunch thyme

2 bay leaves

salt, pepper

1. Cut off the squid heads and tentacles from the body sacs. Coarsely chop the tentacles. Remove and discard any remaining intestines, the eyes, and the beak from the center of the tentacles. Clean out the sacs, taking care not to tear them. Rub off the thin purple covering membrane, rinse well in cold water, and leave to drain.

2. Peel and chop the shallot and garlic. Coarsely chop the chives, basil, and parsley. Cut the crusts from the bread, lightly toast the slices, and make into bread crumbs.

3. Heat the oil. Add the shallot and cook for 3–5 minutes, until softened. Add the squid tentacles and, as soon as they have become opaque, remove from the heat and stir in the bread crumbs, garlic, thyme, and bay leaves. Add the egg and mix to a paste.

4. Preheat the oven to 350°F. Spoon the filling into the squid sacs and secure the openings with a toothpick. Season the bottled strained tomatoes with salt and pepper and add the brandy, thyme, and bay leaves. Place in an ovenproof dish and arrange the squid on top.

5. Cook for 35–40 minutes, turning the squid halfway through the cooking time. Set aside to cool.

TASTE BITE

EXCELLENT WITH SLICES OF BREAD flavored with tomato and sprinkled with olive oil (see step 3 in Catalan-style bread with marinated sea bass recipe, page 62).

TIP

DO NOT OVERFILL the squid sacs or they may burst during cooking. Turn them over with a spatula rather than a fork, which could puncture them.

Mussels in a Spanish marinade

Preparation time:
25 min

Chilling: 3 hours

Cooking time:
10–15 min

Serves 6

**2 pounds large
fresh mussels**

**3$\frac{1}{2}$ tablespoons dry
white wine**

**4 tablespoons
lemon juice**

1 bay leaf

**1 garlic clove,
chopped**

1 red onion

$\frac{1}{2}$ lemon

1 bunch chives

4 mint sprigs

**1 tablespoon pink
peppercorns**

salt, pepper

1. Scrub the mussels under cold, running water and pull off the beards. Discard any with damaged shells or that do not shut immediately when sharply tapped. Put them in a large pan, cover tightly, and cook over low heat, shaking the pan occasionally, until they open, discarding any that remain shut. Take the mussels out of their shells and set aside in a terrine.

2. Drain the cooking liquid (about 1 cup) through a strainer lined with cheesecloth into a clean pan.

3. Add the wine, lemon juice, bay leaf, and garlic to the mussel cooking liquid, season with salt and pepper, and simmer for 5 minutes.

4. Slice the onion into rings. Thinly slice the lemon. Put the onion rings and lemon slices into the terrine with the shelled mussels.

5. Chop the chives and add to the terrine with the mint leaves and the peppercorns. Pour on the boiled marinade, stir well, and leave to cool. Chill for 3 hours.

TIP

YOU COULD TRANSPORT the mussels still in their shells, if you like.

TASTE BITE

VERY GOOD with slices of bread spread with lightly salted butter, or spiced butter (see recipe for red butter, page 36), or with bread flavored with tomato (see step 3 in Catalan-style bread with marinated sea bass recipe, page 62).

Jumbo shrimp marinated in peppered oil

Preparation time:
20 min

Cooking time: 10 min

Marinate: 3 hours

Serves 6

1 bouquet garni

**scant 1 cup white
wine vinegar**

**12 very large
jumbo shrimp**

3 red bell peppers

**2 yellow bell
peppers**

**1 teaspoon cayenne
pepper**

**4 tablespoons olive
oil**

coarse cooking salt

1. Bring $6\frac{1}{4}$ cups water to a boil with a handful of coarse salt and the bouquet garni. Add $\frac{3}{4}$ cup of the white wine vinegar and simmer for 5 minutes, then drop in the shrimp, and cook for about 2–4 minutes according to their size, until they change color. Drain and refresh immediately in cold water. Transfer to a dish.

2. Halve and seed the bell peppers and cut the flesh into strips. Add 1 tablespoon coarse salt and a dash of white wine vinegar to 2 cups water and bring to a boil. Add the bell peppers and cook for 2 minutes, then drain, and refresh in cold water. Transfer to the dish of shrimp.

3. Combine the cayenne with the olive oil and pour the mixture over the shrimp and bell peppers. Leave in a cool place for at least 3 hours.

-☀- TIP

IF FRESH JUMBO SHRIMP are unavailable, use frozen ones, following the thawing instructions carefully before cooking in step 1.

Triple tortilla: piperade, herbs, and cheese

Preparation time:
30 min

Cooking time: 1 hour

Serves 6

For the piperade tortilla

8 ounces each bell peppers and onions

2 garlic cloves

1 slice ham, diced

1 bouquet garni

1 pound tomatoes

2 teaspoons sugar

8 eggs

olive oil

salt, pepper

For the herb tortilla

1 bunch parsley

¹/₂ bunch chives

2 tarragon sprigs

2 garlic cloves

6 eggs

olive oil

salt, pepper

For the cheese tortilla

1²/₃ cups grated romano cheese

1 garlic clove

cayenne pepper

6 eggs

scant 1 cup milk

olive oil

salt, pepper

1. For the piperade, halve and seed the bell peppers and cut the flesh into pieces. Peel and chop the onions. Peel and chop the garlic.

2. Cut off the rind and fat from the ham and cook them in a nonstick skillet until the fat runs. Add the onions, ham, garlic, and bell peppers.

3. Mix thoroughly, add the bouquet garni, and cook gently for 15 minutes. Meanwhile, peel, seed, and chop the tomatoes. Add them to the skillet, season with salt and pepper, and add the sugar. Cook over medium heat until all the water has evaporated. Let cool, then remove the bouquet garni and ham rind.

4. Beat the eggs in a bowl, season with salt and pepper, then stir in the piperade. Heat a little olive oil in an omelet pan and pour in the mixture. When the eggs begin to set, turn the tortilla over, and cook the other side.

5. Make the other two tortillas in the same way, one with the chopped herbs and chopped garlic, the other with the grated romano, chopped garlic, and a pinch of cayenne. For the cheese tortilla, beat the eggs with the milk.

6. Stack the tortillas in layers. When cold, cut into portions and spike each with a toothpick to keep the layers together. Pack in an airtight container to transport to the picnic.

TASTE BITE

EXCELLENT served on large slices of bread. It is also good with potatoes. It is the classic Spanish tortilla—thick and high in fat, but so delicious.

TIP

DON'T STIR THE EGGS during cooking as this will make the omelets more difficult to cut.

Tapas: ham with figs; pancetta with melon; smoked duck breast with apricots

Preparation time:
20 min, 2 hours
before

6 fresh figs

6 apricots

1 melon

3¹/₂ ounces smoked duck breast

12 slices round pancetta

6 slices lean ham

1. Cut the figs and apricots into fourths. Halve the melon and remove the seeds, then cut into fourths.

2. Remove the melon rind and cut the flesh into pieces. Chill all the fruit in the refrigerator for 2 hours.

3. Cut off the fat from the duck breast and the rind from the ham. With toothpicks, spear pieces of duck breast to the apricot fourths, the pancetta to the melon, and folded pieces of the ham to the figs.

TIP

ALL THE TAPAS can be placed on a slice of crusty baguette or ciabatta.

Tartlets with ricotta and cheese filling

Preparation time:
20 min

Chilling: 2 hours

Cooking time: 25 min

Serves 6

For the dough

1¼ cups all-purpose flour

1 vanilla bean

½ cup butter

salt

For the filling

3½ ounces Manchego cheese (or a good medium-hard cheese)

5 tablespoons butter

4 eggs, separated

¾ cups superfine sugar

2 tablespoons cornstarch

1 cup ricotta cheese

½ cup sour cream

grated rind of 1 lemon

1. To make the dough, sift the flour with a pinch of salt into a mixing bowl. Split the vanilla bean, scrape out the black seeds, and add to the flour.

2. Dice the butter, add to the flour, and rub in lightly with your fingertips. Gradually add 2–3 tablespoons ice water and mix to a dough. Form into a ball, wrap in plastic wrap, and chill for 2 hours.

3. Preheat the oven to 350°F. Roll out the dough on a lightly floured counter and line six muffin pans.

4. For the filling, shave the cheese into thin slivers with a vegetable peeler. Melt the butter over low heat.

5. Whisk the egg yolks with the sugar until pale and fluffy, then add the cornstarch, ricotta, sour cream, butter, and lemon rind.

6. In a separate bowl, whisk the egg whites to stiff peaks and gently fold into the egg yolk mixture. Fill the tartlet cases and sprinkle with half the cheese slivers. Bake for 25 minutes. Sprinkle the remaining cheese over the tartlets as soon as they come out of the oven.

TASTE BITE
DELICIOUS accompanied by a sharp fruit jelly—quince. if it is available.

country

parks

Cottage cheese with herbs and white wine on crusty bread

Preparation time:
15 min

Draining time:
1 hour

Serves 6

2 cups cottage cheese

2 scallions

1 white shallot

$1/_2$ bunch each flat leaf parsley, chives, and chervil

1 thyme sprig

3 tablespoons white wine

1 teaspoon sherry vinegar

1 teaspoon olive oil

$1/_2$ cup mascarpone cheese

salt, pepper

1. Put the cottage cheese into a strainer and leave to drain for 1 hour. Peel and chop the scallions and shallot. Chop the herbs briefly in a processor or herb mill.

2. Mash the cottage cheese with a fork, then beat it with a spatula until it is smooth. Add the scallions, shallot, and herbs and season to taste with salt and pepper.

3. Stir in the white wine, sherry vinegar, and olive oil. Leave in a cool place for 2 hours.

4. Whisk the mascarpone and stir it into the flavored cottage cheese. Serve on slices of fresh baguette.

Duck terrine

Preparation time:
45 min,
1 or 2 days before

Cooking time:
1¹/₂ hours

Serves 6

1 oven-ready duck

5 ounces side of pork

10 ounces lean pork

1 eating apple

6 prunes

3 tablespoons brandy or calvados

1 teaspoon pepper

1 pound duck breasts

coarse salt

fine salt

TASTE BITE
EXCELLENT on slices of coarse country bread, with a few leaves of arugula and pickles.

TIP
THE PRUNES could be replaced by mushrooms. Make sure that you include a good proportion of fat in the ingredients.

1. Preheat the oven to 350°F. Skin the duck and cut off the breast meat. Remove the legs and bone them. Cut the breast and leg meat (about 10 ounces) into small cubes.

2. Coarsely chop both kinds of pork meat and grind it in a food processor, using the pulse control so as not to overheat the mixture. Peel and core the apple and chop finely. Pit the prunes and cut into pieces.

3. Add the apple, diced duck meat, brandy, coarse salt, and pepper to the pork mixture.

4. Skin the duck breasts and cut into strips. Season with salt.

5. Spread a layer of the duck and pork mixture in the base of a terrine and press down well. Cover with strips of duck breast and a few pieces of prune. Continue to layer the remaining ingredients in the same way.

6. Put the terrrine, uncovered, in a roasting pan half-filled with hot water and bake for 1¹/₂ hours. Remove the terrine and set aside to cool. When still just lukewarm, cover with foil-wrapped cardboard and place a weight on top. Chill until the next day. Keep in the terrine to take to the picnic.

Chicken and eggplant flan

Preparation time:
45 min the previous
day or 2 hours
in advance

Cooking time: 35 min

Serves 6

For the dough

1¼ cups all-purpose flour

scant ½ cup butter

salt

For the filling

3 large chicken breast portions, skinned and boned

3 thyme sprigs

3 bay leaves

olive oil, for drizzling

scant ½ cup tapenade (see page 125)

1 jar eggplant preserved in oil

salt

-ğ- TIP

IF SHORT OF TIME, use 8 ounces of ready-made shortcrust pastry.

1. For the dough, sift the flour with a pinch of salt into a mixing bowl. Dice the butter, add to the flour, and lightly rub in with your fingertips.

2. Gradually add 1–2 tablespoons water to bind into a dough, handling the pastry as little as possible. Form into a ball and chill in the refrigerator.

3. Preheat the oven to 400°F.

4. Oil three rectangles of kitchen foil and place one chicken breast portion on each. Season with salt and pepper and top with a sprig of thyme and a bay leaf. Drizzle with olive oil.

5. Fold the foil over and seal the edges to make three packages. Place on a cookie sheet and bake for 15 minutes. Check that the chicken is cooked by inserting the point of a sharp knife; if the juices run clear, it is ready.

6. Grease and flour an 8-inch quiche pan. Roll out the dough on a lightly floured surface and line the pan, pressing the dough to exclude trapped air, then prick the base all over with a fork. Bake for 15–20 minutes. Remove from the oven and, when cool, spread the tapenade over the base.

7. Drain the eggplant on paper towels. Remove the chicken breast portions from the foil and cut into slices. Fill the pie shell, alternating slices of meat with the eggplant.

Mushroom packets

Preparation time:
20 min

Cooking time: 30 min

Serves 6

24 large white mushrooms

1/2 lemon

3 slices bread

3 basil sprigs

1 bunch flat leaf parsley

1 bunch chives

7 ounces ham

1 egg, beaten

3 tablespoons sour cream

3 1/2 tablespoons Madeira or muscatel (or other sweet dessert wine)

olive oil, for brushing

salt, pepper

TASTE BITE

EAT THE PACKETS COLD with a few drops of ketchup or Tabasco.

TIP

TO MAKE THE PACKETS EASIER to transport and pretty to look at, blanch some long chive leaves for 2 seconds in boiling water to soften them and use them to tie the mushroom packets together neatly.

1. Preheat the oven to 350°F. Remove the mushroom stems and slightly enlarge the cavity in the cups to make room for the stuffing. Rub them over with the cut side of the lemon.

2. For the stuffing, lightly toast the bread and crush into bread crumbs. Chop the basil, parsley, and chives.

3. Remove any rind from the ham and chop the meat in a food processor. Combine the bread crumbs with the egg, ham, 4 tablespoons of chopped herbs, the sour cream, and the wine. Season with salt and pepper.

4. Brush all the mushroom caps with olive oil and season to taste with salt and pepper.

5. Fill 12 of the mushroom caps with the stuffing and cover with the remaining 12 caps. Place on a cookie sheet and bake for 25–30 minutes, until they are browned and the stuffing is firm. Leave to cool.

Wild mushroom turnovers

Preparation time:
25 min

Cooking time: 50 min

Serves 6
(2 turnovers)

1¹/₂ pounds mixed wild or cultivated mushrooms (shiitake, oyster, cremini, etc.)

2 small leeks

2 tablespoons butter

1 tablespoon rice flour

4 tablespoons sour cream

1 tablespoon port

2 puff pastry dough rounds, thawed if frozen

1 egg, beaten

salt, pepper

1. Preheat the oven to 400°F. Cut the mushrooms into pieces, season with salt, and cook in a covered sauté pan, over medium heat, for 5 minutes. Drain and reserve the cooking liquid.

2. Cut the leeks into rings. Melt the butter in a pan and cook the leeks gently over low heat for 10 minutes. Add the mushrooms, season with pepper, and cook for 5 minutes, or until they have browned.

3. Mix the rice flour into the reserved cooking liquid, add the sour cream and port, and cook in a small pan for about 1 minute to thicken. Gently stir into the leek and mushroom mixture.

4. Lay the rounds of pastry dough on the counter and spread the filling over one half of each. Fold the other half of the dough over to form a semicircle, seal, and crimp the edges. Brush the top with beaten egg to glaze. Place on a cookie sheet and bake for about 25 minutes, until puffed up and golden.

TASTE BITE

GOOD HOT OR COLD. These are equally delicious made with ceps, which need no preliminary sweating. Simply slice them and lightly cook for 15 minutes. Adding rice flour to the sour cream is also unnecessary, as the ceps contain a natural thickening agent.

TIP

IF YOU WANT to keep these turnovers hot, wrap them first in kitchen foil and then several layers of newspaper, which is an excellent insulator.

Harvester's terrine

Preparation time:
30 min, 2 days
before

Cooking time:
2³/₄ hours

Serves 6

**1 pound lean
pork side, cut
into slices**

**1¹/₂ pounds beef
shank**

2 bay leaves

2 garlic cloves

**¹/₄ teaspoon Sichuan
pepper (or ground
mixed peppercorns)**

1 bottle red wine

2 onions

2 carrots

olive oil

2 cloves

1 bouquet garni

3 gelatin leaves

**2 tablespoons
chopped parsley**

salt, pepper

For the sauce

**1 candied orange
rind**

3 pickles

1 cup mayonnaise

**1 tablespoon
chopped parsley**

TASTE BITE

FRIED POLENTA makes a
pleasant change from bread
to eat with this dish.

1. Two days prior to serving, put the meat into a bowl, add the bay leaves, garlic, and Sichuan pepper. Pour in enough wine to cover the meat. Cover the bowl and leave to marinate in the refrigerator until the following day.

2. Preheat the oven to 350°F. Drain the meat, reserving the marinade with the bay leaves and garlic. Halve the onions and cut the carrots into chunks.

3. Heat the oil in a large skillet and brown the meat for 10 minutes, season with salt and pepper, and transfer to an ovenproof dish. Cook the carrots and onions in the oil left in the pan for 5 minutes, then add to the meat.

4. Add the reserved marinade, cloves, bouquet garni, and remaining wine. Season with salt. Cover tightly with foil and cook for 2¹/₂ hours, or until tender.

5. Take out the meat and strain the cooking liquid into a bowl. Soak the gelatin in cold water until soft, then squeeze it dry, and add to the hot cooking liquid. Stir until dissolved.

6. Cut the meat into cubes and combine with the chopped parsley. Place the meat in a terrine, pour the liquid over it and chill until the next day.

7. For the sauce, finely chop the orange peel and pickles and combine with the mayonnaise and parsley.

Fruit and vanilla tart

Preparation time:
25 min, 3 hours
in advance

Cooking time: 25 min

Serves 6

For the sweet pie dough

2 cups all-purpose flour

³/₄ cup confectioners' sugar

²/₃ cup softened butter

1 egg

salt

For the filling

1 pound fruit, such as blueberries, black currants, plums, etc.

¹/₃ cup sugar, or more according to sweetness of fruit

¹/₂ vanilla bean

60 lady finger cookies

confectioners' sugar

1. To make the dough, sift the flour and a pinch of salt into a large bowl. Sprinkle with the sugar, then rub in the butter with your fingertips until the mixture resembles coarse bread crumbs. Make a well in the center, break the egg into it, and begin mixing, with your fingers, bringing the flour from the sides to the center. Quickly form the mixture into a ball and let rest for about 3 hours in a cool place.

2. Preheat the oven to 400°F. Roll out the dough on a floured counter and line a pie pan.

3. Rinse and prepare your chosen fruit. Drain on paper towels and put in a bowl with the sugar. Mix well. Slit the vanilla bean, scrape out the seeds, and combine with the fruit.

4. Crush the cookies and sprinkle on the base of the pie shell. Arrange the fruit on top and bake for 25 minutes. While the tart is still just warm, dredge it with confectioners' sugar.

Fall fruit salad

Preparation time:
25 min

Chilling: 2 hours

Cooking time: 10 min

Serves 6

1 lemon

**1 bottle sweet
white wine**

¹/₄ cup sugar

**2 star anise seed
pods**

6 dried apricots

6 pitted prunes

3 apples

3 pears

**1 large bunch of
sweet grapes**

**¹/₂ cup walnut
halves**

1. Pare a thin strip of rind from the lemon. Pour the wine into a pan, add the sugar, and bring to a boil, then add the lemon rind and star anise.

2. Cook gently for 5 minutes, then remove the pan from the heat. Add the apricots and prunes and leave to soak while the liquid cools. Pour into a bowl.

3. Squeeze the lemon juice. Peel, core, and slice the apples and pears. Halve and, if necessary, seed the grapes; sprinkle with the lemon juice; and add the apples, pears, and grapes to the apricots and prunes. Add the walnuts and stir well. Chill for 2 hours.

TASTE BITE

ADD A LITTLE CHOPPED MINT just before serving this dessert at your picnic. and remember to take along some lady finger cookies to eat with it.

TIP

THE INGREDIENTS of this easy-to-prepare fruit salad can be varied with the seasons: cherries and strawberries in the spring. peaches and apricots in the summer.

a pause
on the
ski
slopes

Tabbouleh with dried fruit

Preparation time:
40 min

Cooking time: 10 min

Serves 6

2¹/₂ cups coarse
couscous

1 bunch mint

1 large bunch
flat leaf parsley

6 dried apricots

2 tablespoons
shelled walnuts

¹/₂ cup raisins

grated nutmeg

¹/₂ cup lemon juice

4 tablespoons olive
oil

salt, pepper

TASTE BITE

IT IS THE QUALITY of the
fresh herbs that gives this
dish its delicious flavor. A
few pistachio nuts may also
be added.

TIP

IF IT CAN BE FOUND in
specialist shops, quinoa,
known as Inca rice, is the
best grain for this recipe. It
is a South American cereal,
similar to coarse, grayish-
brown couscous. It has a
higher protein content than
wheat (15%) and is used in
sweet and savory dishes.

1. Cook the couscous according to the
packet instructions.

2. Chop the mint and the parsley. Cut
the apricots into small pieces and
coarsely chop the walnuts.

3. When the couscous is cooked, leave
it to rest for 10 minutes in a bowl
before stirring it and checking there
are no lumps. Add the apricots,
walnuts, raisins, and herbs. Mix well
and season with pepper and a good
pinch of nutmeg.

4. Combine the lemon juice and olive
oil and stir into the tabbouleh.

Ham, apple, and raisin strudel

Preparation time:
25 min

Cooking time: 30 min

Serves 4
(2 strudels)

3 large apples

$1/4$ cup butter

1–2 tablespoons sugar

8 sheets phyllo pastry

4 thin slices ham (Aosta or prosciutto)

2 tablespoons raisins

$1/2$ cup walnut halves

ground cinnamon

confectioners' sugar

TASTE BITE

EAT THE STRUDELS HOT OR JUST WARM. To keep them hot, store them wrapped in newspaper, inside an insulated bag.

TIP

STRUDEL is a sweet pastry of Austrian origin. In this savory version the salt and sugar make a completely wonderful combination.

1. Peel, core, and slice the apples and put in a pan with half of the butter, the sugar, and enough water just to cover the base of the pan. Cook gently for about 10 minutes, until the apples are soft but not reduced to pulp. Remove from the heat and let cool.

2. Preheat the oven to 350°F.

3. Melt the remaining butter. Lay one sheet of phyllo pastry on the counter and brush it with the melted butter. Lay a second sheet on top of the first, brush with melted butter, and then add a third.

4. Lay two slices of ham on the pastry and spread with half the apple. Sprinkle half the raisins and nuts over the apple, leaving a 1-inch border of pastry all around. Prepare the second strudel with three of the remaining sheets of phyllo and the rest of the filling.

5. Carefully roll each strudel into a log shape. Dampen the edges and place them on a cookie sheet. Brush the last two sheets of phyllo with melted butter, crumple them, and lay them on top of the strudels. Sprinkle with cinnamon and confectioners' sugar and bake for 20 minutes.

Pick-me-up soup

Preparation time:
25 min

Cooking time: 35 min

Serves 6

3 potatoes

2 shallots

2 celery stalks

3 carrots

2 leeks

2 tablespoons olive oil, plus extra

1 tablespoon fresh ginger root, chopped

1²/₃ cups pearl barley, rinsed

1 thyme sprig

¹/₂ bunch chervil, chopped

salt, pepper

◎ TASTE BITE

FOR THE SAKE OF SIMPLICITY, the carrots may be diced and cooked together with the potatoes. Only the leeks then need to be added later.

☼ TIP

BARLEY IS RICH IN calcium, phosphorus, and potassium. For ease of cooking the husked grains are passed between two millstones. The resulting "pearl" barley is then prepared in the same way as rice.

1. Dice the potatoes and chop the shallots. Thinly slice the celery and shave the carrot into thin strips with a vegetable peeler. Slice the leeks.

2. Heat 2 tablespoons of olive oil in a heavy pan.

3. Gently cook the shallots, add the potatoes and ginger, and season with salt and pepper. Stir well and gradually add 7¹/₂ cups water. Bring to a boil and add the pearl barley, thyme, and celery. Cover, lower the heat, and simmer for 15 minutes.

4. Add the leeks and carrot to the soup. Continue cooking for 10 more minutes, then adjust the seasoning, if necessary, and stir in a few drops of olive oil. Chop the chervil leaves and stir into the soup.

5. Remove the thyme and pour the soup into an insulated container where it will keep hot until needed.

Blue cheese and pear tartlets

Preparation time:
20 min

Cooking time: 8 min

Serves 6

**1 pack puff pastry,
thawed if frozen**

3 ripe pears

**2 tablespoons lemon
juice**

**10 ounces soft
blue-veined cheese**

**1 tablespoon sour
cream**

butter

1. Preheat the oven to 425°F. Roll out the pastry, cut into rounds and line six muffin pans, leaving a little overhang as the pastry will shrink slightly while cooking. Set aside in the refrigerator.

2. Peel, core, and thinly slice the pears. Sprinkle the slices with lemon juice to prevent discoloration.

3. Mash the cheese with a fork and combine with the sour cream. Divide this between the tartlets and arrange the strips of pear on the top. Bake for 7–8 minutes.

 TIP

TO ARRIVE INTACT, these tartlets need to travel in their pans so, for preference, use lightweight aluminum foil cases, from which the tartlets slip easily—ready to serve.

Cortina d'Ampezzo open sandwiches

Preparation time:
20 minutes,
1 hour in advance

Serves 6

For the nut butter

¹/₄ cup walnut halves

¹/₄ cup butter

For the sandwiches

18 slices various types of salami and ham

3¹/₂ ounces young spinach leaves

2 ounces arugula

7 ounces Parmesan cheese

scant ¹/₂ cup ricotta cheese

2 sliced loaves

pepper

1. To make the walnut butter, finely grind the walnuts in a food processor and mix with the softened butter. Leave to set in a cool place for 1 hour.

2. Remove the rinds from the meat. Strip the stems from the spinach leaves and arugula. Shave thin slices from the Parmesan with a vegetable peeler.

3. Mash the ricotta with a fork and spread on half of the bread slices. Spread the remaining slices with the walnut butter.

4. Place the Parmesan shavings and the arugula leaves on one half of the slices spread with ricotta and the spinach and ham on the other half of the slices.

5. Top the slices spread with walnut butter with the remaining meat and a few spinach or arugula leaves.

TIP

WALNUT BUTTER HAS a delicious flavor when spread on sliced bread. Use it for sandwiches made with Cheddar and similar hard cheeses, as well as Gorgonzola, Dolcelatte, or Bresse Bleu, together with a few fresh salad greens. Hazelnuts or cashews can also be used to flavor butter.

Cookie sandwiches

Preparation time:
10 min

Cooking time:
6–7 min

Serves 4

For the cookies

scant 1/2 cup butter

1 1/4 cups all-purpose flour

2 egg yolks

5 tablespoons confectioners' sugar

1 teaspoon baking powder

2 teaspoons grated fresh ginger root

confectioners' sugar, for dusting

For the filling

generous 1/2 cup shelled hazelnuts

1 can sweetened chestnut purée

1. Preheat the oven to 350°F. To make the cookies, soften the butter to room temperature. Put the flour in a mixing bowl and rub in the butter until the mixture resembles coarse bread crumbs. Set aside.

2. In another bowl, whisk the egg yolks with the sugar until pale and fluffy, then add the flour mixture, baking powder, and ginger. Combine by hand and form into a ball. Set aside in a cool place for 20 minutes.

3. Roll out the dough on a counter dusted with confectioners' sugar to a thickness of 1/4 inch. Cut into triangles with a sharp knife.

4. Place the cookies on a nonstick cookie sheet and bake for about 6–7 minutes, until the edges are browned. Using a metal spatula, transfer to a wire rack to cool.

5. For the filling, coarsely chop the hazelnuts. Just before serving, spread the chestnut purée evenly on half the cookies and sprinkle on the chopped nuts. Top with the remaining cookies to make sandwiches.

◉ TASTE BITE

TOP THE COOKIE SANDWICHES with a cloud of whipped cream (an aerosol can weighs very little in your backpack).

Wine mulled with orange and cinnamon

Preparation time: 10 min

Cooking time: 5 min

Serves 6

1 orange, unwaxed or well scrubbed

1 cinnamon stick

1 bottle red wine

6 brown sugar lumps

2 cloves

6 peppercorns

1. Pare a long, thin strip of rind from the orange, taking care to avoid the pith. Break the cinnamon stick into several pieces.

2. Put the wine into a pan with the orange rind, cinnamon, sugar, cloves, and peppercorns and place over low heat. If you wish to retain the alcohol content, do not let it boil; otherwise let it simmer gently for 10 minutes to diffuse the spicy aromas. Put it in a vacuum flask until required.

TIP

USE A FULL-BODIED WINE, such as a Côtes-du-Rhône, Corbière or a Coteau-du-Languedoc.

TASTE BITE

EXCELLENT to drink with hot chestnuts or with Pine nut tart (see page 70) and Fruit and vanilla tart (see page 105).

Ten tips for a successful picnic

1. Don't forget to pack a can opener, a sharp knife, and a corkscrew—or a Swiss army knife that performs all these functions.

2. Remember to pack paper napkins, plenty of paper plates (as you need a layer of 2–3 per person to make a steady plate), and a roll of paper towels.

3. Take along some garbage bags in the interests of keeping the countryside tidy.

4. Store all the prepared items in airtight containers, insulated jars, or cold bags (especially in hot weather, when things dry out very quickly).

5. Wrap sandwiches in plastic wrap or foil to keep the fillings from escaping.

6. Pack tartlets and small prepared dishes in insulated bags, boxes, or baskets to make sure they do not rattle around.

7. Pack the most fragile ingredients on the top of less delicate items: putting a terrine on top of hard-cooked eggs and tomatoes is not a good idea!

8. Leave flans in the dishes they were cooked in. Aluminum foil dishes are ideal as they are light to carry and disposable.

9. Remember to take full water bottles. In hot weather you need at least a $2\frac{1}{2}$ cups per person. And don't forget the disposable drinking cups. Plastic nets, too, are useful for cooling bottles of wine or water in the river, but be sure to anchor them well or you may see your drinks floating away on the current!

10. A vacuum flask for tea, coffee, or mulled wine is absolutely indispensable in wintertime.

Basic recipes

PASTRY AND DOUGH

Shortcrust dough (p. 98): The classic pastry dough for quiches and vegetable flans

Sweet shortcrust pastry (p. 70): Ideal for all fruit tarts

Bread dough (p. 63): It is easy to make in a food processor but needs to be left to rise, or the result will be hard and brittle. It is the ideal base for pissaladière, pizza, and some open sandwiches. Supermarkets stock pizza bases and semibaked bread rolls, just needing a final bake at home.

Sweet pie dough (p. 105): An alternative classic recipe to use when making fruit tarts and crispy toppings.

TIP
BUTTERING THE BREAD helps to keep sandwiches moist. It also enhances the flavors. Mayonnaise bought in tubes or jars is indeed easy to transport, but home-made mayonnaise is so much nicer and can be flavored in many ways: with garlic, herbs, condiments, spices, etc.

SAUCES

Red butter (p. 36): For open sandwiches based on raw, smoked, or cooked fish.

Walnut butter (p. 117): A high-calorie spread that is perfect in sandwiches after a long fall or winter hike. It is especially tasty with a selection of cold meats.

Herb mayonnaise (p. 34)

Tartar sauce (p. 10): Ideal with crudités, roasts, and cold chicken.

Guacamole (p. 10): Ready-made versions are often acid and contain too much garlic. Good guacamole is delicious with Mexican tacos or on pita pockets.

Cottage cheese with herbs (p. 10): For open sandwiches and crudités.

Mint sauce (p. 48): For use with all cold meats, especially lamb.

Tapenade (pp. 67, 98): A thick paste made from capers, anchovies, olives, olive oil, lemon juice, and seasoning. Commercial varieties in jars are widely available.

TIP
READY-MADE pastry dough bought from the supermarket is very practical. There is no need to make puff pastry, unless you really like to, but other kinds take only a few minutes to prepare in a food processor or even by hand.

fishing trips and lakesides

out of town

a day on the river

beaches and sand dunes

beneath the pines

a pause on the ski slopes

country parks

This book first published by EPA, a division of
Hachette-Livre, 43 Quai de Grenelle,
Paris 75905, Cedex 15, France.

© 2001 EPA – Hachette-Livre, Paris
under the title Pique-Niques

Language translation produced by Translate-A-Book,
Oxford

Typesetting: Organ Graphic, Abingdon

© 2003 English translation, Octopus Publishing
Group Ltd, London

This edition published by Hachette Illustrated UK,
Octopus Publishing Group, 2–4 Heron Quays,
London E14 4JP

Editor
Joan Le Boru

Artistic design
Nancy Dorking

Layout
Nadine Gautier-Quentin

Platemaking: Eurésys, à Baisieux

Printing: Tien Wah Press, Singapore

Registration of copyright: 09540 – June 2001

ISBN : 1-84430-023-4